The Practical Guide to Applying The Law Of Attraction

Anthea Morphitis

Copyright © 2018 by Anthea Morphitis.

All rights reserved. No part of this publication may be reproduced, distributed or transmitted in any form or by any means, including photocopying, recording, or other electronic or mechanical methods, without the prior written permission of the publisher, except in the case of brief quotations embodied in critical reviews and certain other noncommercial uses permitted by copyright law.

Urlaw - The Practical Guide to Applying The Law Of Attraction / Anthea Morphitis. —1st ed.

ISBN 978-1-9164870-0-0

ACKNOWLEDGEMENTS

Firstly I would like to say thank you to you, my reader, for picking up this book, probably in the hope of finally gaining clarity on how exactly to apply The Law of Attraction 1.

I, as the author, am very happy as this means you're ready to take on the content that is presented to you and start to implement the steps that we have created, not only from months of research but also through years of personal experiences.

This book then has been created to help you achieve all the great things that you may (or may not) know you are capable of achieving; for this, I am truly excited as we embark on this glorious journey together!

I would also like to express my deepest appreciation to Andre Marcos 2 founder of Vercov Consultancy 3, who has now become part of my executive leadership team and is the person who sat down with me and supported my thinking at the blank paper stage and has continued to support driving Urlaw™ forward to the book you now have in your hands.

He has not only been part of the initial team, but also a great friend, leader, and a phenomenal coach. I want to say thank you for his willingness to share his time so generously, for having faith, and believing in the idea of Urlaw™, for without his input, strategies and constant motivation, I would not be here talking to you from these pages today, so thank you!

I would also like to express my deepest appreciation to Esther Hicks also known as Abraham Hicks, as all my work has and still is inspired by her teachings of The Law of Attraction. Her work has taken my mind and my life to another level, without her easy to reach material I surely would not be in the position I am today and for that I am truly internally grateful. Thank you!

About the Author: Anthea Morphitis

BELIEF.EXPERIENCE.FACT

Let me share a couple of insights into what makes Anthea tick and is most passionate about, first off all she loves nothing more than helping people make the progressive movement towards attracting those things that they want in their lives. Secondly, she also loves to indulge in Self-Development, for she believes and has had first-hand personal experience of the fact that we are either our own best friend or our own worst enemy. Sometimes, as you will come to realise these series of thoughts that we have, (which might not even be our own thoughts) are the only things locking, blocking and holding back the life we desire, we deserve, and we are here to lead.

> *The biggest realization that Anthea come to, was, life is what we think, our beliefs, and how we feel, although this is a book about 'The Law of Attraction' you will realise that it's really about YOU, the way YOU think, the way YOU feel and the perspective YOU hold on yourself and others.*

Anthea has a couple of key jobs; priority number one is that she's a mother of two and somebody who, perhaps like yourself, has experienced many turbulences in their life. This required her to search for solutions and answers, in a way anything, something that could help her to be able to get through, under, over or around the other side of it. IT being the present situation and set of circumstances that she found herself in at that exact place, headspace and point in time.

With her personal Development Coach hat on, Anthea works from home where she runs her Coaching and Personal Development Company Urlaw™, she's a published Author and a Speaker. This has afforded her a great deal of experience in helping not only other people but also, and perhaps, more importantly, herself having gone through the process of supporting, nurturing and healing herself and manifested the life that she attracted through design.

> **'Stress and Unhappiness come not from situations, but how you respond to situations'** *Brian Tracy*

I actually got started in the Coaching and Personal Development industry through a certain specific set of events that lead to a crystallisation of a thought process that I had already been practicing, however it was never crystal and never clear. After experiencing trial and tribulation which ended up in being homeless with my children on more than one occasion, being exposed to the book 'The Secret' and Law of Attraction crystallised the way I was thinking and made it much more of an occurring positive approach to handling things rather than accepting defeat. This actually gave me, more convection and more power, it pretty much upped my energy and my ability to make things happen because I was thinking them! This lead to thinking "If I am getting results like this, then I want to share them" I was inspired and felt compelled to write a book titled 'Feel Good And Watch What Happens" which is about my personal life experiences, Law of Attraction and how having a positive mental attitude actually generates positive emotions, thoughts, and experiences. As a result it has opened the doors to the industry, because people were inspired and motivated by what they had read, and had I not had those experiences, I would never of know I was able to make the strides that I have made, which lead me to want to write this book, as I didn't want anybody else to waste time not knowing how to apply "The Law of Attraction".

> *'Never be afraid to fall apart. It presents an opportunity to rebuild yourself the way you'd been all along'* - Kushandwizdom

I hold a number of values, and one of those values is Love, and it's not any kind of love because there are multiple types of love, I am talking about self-love and self-respect because they lead you in my process to a number of significant things. So being put on my own, if I didn't maintain one of my own values of 'Love' for myself or 'Respect' for myself, I would have fallen from the middle of the earth.

> *"If we're not just judging ourselves based on our accomplishments it means that we can have respect for ourselves aside from what we manage to have, do or require."* - Anthea Morphitis

Foreword

Firstly, let me introduce myself (so as not to be rude).

My name is Tyrone Curtis Wade; I am a 37-year-old father of three healthy, but extremely cheeky children (two boys and a girl) and a proud member of the human race. I recently graduated with a 1st BSc Honors degree from Anglia Ruskin University, in Business, Management, and Healthcare.

Anthea Morphitis (or more sweeties as I affectionately refer to her) is not one of my most extended friends. This being said, Anthea is one of my most valued, partly due to her sheer determination and ability to let her life be an example of truth, forgiveness, and discovery. More Sweeties, surpasses the notion of wearing one's heart on their sleeve, by allowing, inviting and thus choosing to attract into her experience of life, the most beautiful and fulfilling situations and opportunities.

One of Anthea's most distinguishable and unique reflections of her character lays in her ability to connect with people and their life experiences from a simplistic, honest yet holistic point of view. More Sweeties entered into my life during a period that I'd been earnestly calling out to experience true inner beauty within humanity, although it took me longer than I would have preferred, my calls were answered when Anthea and myself became friends. Anthea exhibited forgiveness and love in ways I'd never seen or perceived and in doing (being) so demonstrated to me and others critical (at the time) of her life choices. She proved it is indeed possible for one to attract into their lives, that which they desire, if only we would allow ourselves (like Anthea has enabled herself) to be open to the wonder called life and the experience of ourselves, by being aware of our creative energy and focus on attract inner peace and acceptance.

I believe F. Scott Fitgerald offers a description of the infections abilities inner beauty has on others, once indeed witnessed.

"She was beautiful, but not like those girls in the magazines. She was beautiful, for the way she thought. She was beautiful, for the sparkle in her eyes when she talked about something she loved. She was beautiful, for her ability to make other people smile, even if she was sad. No, she wasn't beautiful for something as temporary as her looks. She was beautiful, deep down to her soul. She is beautiful."

— F. Scott Fitzgerald

Furthermore, the source of Anthea's inner beauty and strength, reside in her ability to cause others also to experience their own inner beauty and power, whether that be on a personal, professional or spiritual individual level. Anthea's unique set of skills, most of which are a part of her natural character, but some she has been forced to cultivate partly due to environmental issues in her early and late teens, have in my opinion amazingly aligned with her character traits and proved to be the most effective when assisting others.

Like most of you who have chosen to pick up this fantastic book, as well as embarking on your own personal journeys you will also be taking part in a global awakening, as have I when I began reading Anthea's book. The Practical Guide to The Law of Attraction does what it says on the tin, it gives an individual the tools needed to guide them through what is and will always be a continuous journey of self-realization and self-discovery, by attracting what they desire rather than what is expected or worst still, what they fear.

You will put it down for two weeks, a day, a month. But the whole time you'll be contemplating on and implementing Anthea Morphitis Practical Guide to The Law of Attraction. Plus… this book makes one always, in all ways want to grab it and go back in for more.

Happy Attracting...

Tyrone Curtis Wade

Contents

ACKNOWLEDGEMENTS iii
About the Author: Anthea Morphitis ii
Foreword vii
Introduction 1
How to use this book 4
Research 6
What it is, What it's not and What it takes 13
Step 1 - Define 17
What Doing Define Looks Like - Exercises: 27
Step 2 - Demand 30
What Doing Demand Looks Like - Exercise 36
Step 3 - Commit 39
What Doing Commit Looks Like - Exercise: 45
Step 4 - Operate 50
What Doing Operate Looks Like - Exercises 56
Step 5 - Appreciate 59
What Doing Appreciate Looks Like - Exercise 65
Step 6- Wait 71
What Doing Wait Looks Like - Exercises: 77
Recap 79
How Does The Law of Attraction Work? Questions and Answers 88

Introduction

This book was written with the pure intent to simplify and guide people through the most popular method that many people are aware of, however, struggle with understanding and applying which is called The Law of Attraction. This is about, living life with motive, purpose, and commitment and making a difference to yourself and others, growing your self-awareness, appreciating and achieving your goals and desires.

We wanted to put something out there in a consumable way, allowing us to reach out to people on a global level. We have found over the years that there is a lot of people that have come across 'The Law of Attraction' and the book 'The Secret,' however, are disenfranchised with it, started it, seen the potential and not really been able to get what they need out of it. We are here to be able to reach out Globally to all of those people, they're not just living in London, Essex or Birmingham there is a worldwide audience of people that are trying to employ and deploy this whilst making it work, and it is not working for them; I don't want them to lose ground, lose focus, lose hope and lose traction, this is their lives! What we have done is simplified it through our 6 step System, helping people get into the right mindset to be able to really Structure, Organize and Get in control of accomplishing the things that they want to out of life!

Also to really understand, apply and achieve the great things that so many know they are capable of achieving but just can't make happen. The Urlaw™ system can be applied to all areas of life, and we've also found that the people who have been applying our steps are getting really incredible life-changing results, so now it is time to share it with everyone else!

> *The first simple rule in life: If you don't go after what you want, you'll never have it.* Author, Unknown

Whilst developing The Company Urlaw™, I was going through some challenging times myself, however, I applied the steps and principles that we're sharing with you here and used them as a springboard for me to actually create The Urlaw™ Book, now in your hands, in either physical or digital form!

> *I'm thankful for my struggles because, without it, I wouldn't have stumbled across my strengths* - Alexandra Elle - Author of Neon Soul: A Collection of Poetry and Prose

The fact that I have studied, practiced and qualified myself as a Law of Attraction practitioner over the past 9 years has ignited a passion for helping others know what I know, So this book isn't for people who don't know about 'The Secret', but it is for people who do know about 'The Secret' and The Law of Attraction and have read the book or watched the DVD, however are struggling to get defined, quantifiable results, struggling to get what they want from it, and want to have a personal take on how I went from homeless and broke to living an abundant, balanced and satisfying life, using these steps in all areas of life.

Urlaw™ is not teaching you 'The Secret,' and it's not teaching you 'The Law of Attraction', It is giving you my insights, years of research and my perception of what you need to know on top of 'The Secret' to make it work for you and highlighting how to use it, using simple steps!

> *I choose to make the rest of my life, the best of my life* - Louise Hays

How to use this book

This book comprises of 6 key Principles that are around that foundation and directly lead on to 18 specific action points that you need to be able to do, and if you do each of these 18 things and you are aware of the 6 principles that guide you through the actions, you're going to get better results from the things you are looking to accomplish helping you really start making progress with The Law of Attraction. Feel free to scan through to gain the impression of the content, making sure you cover the 3 W's of What it is, What it's not and What it Takes, and then you can get started when you are ready.

You will find out that this book is filled with analogies helping you to understand the process and inspirational quotes that I find motivating and inspiring and hope you resonate with them too. As you work through this book; at the end of each chapter, you will find exercises and action steps. That we have set in a strategic order for you to follow. You will need to invest in a couple of notepads to take notes and for specific steps and be ready and willing to put time, focus and energy when implementing the steps. We have also provided space at the end of the exercises so you can get started straight away, and we have also included extra blank pages at the back of the book, in order for you to use for any further notes if needed.

This is a straightforward, simple system and easy to use, giving structure that if applied correctly will help change things for you. I truly hope that you embrace the content, follow the steps and be well on your way to gaining clarity and feeling good about Who you are, where you are, and the direction you are going, ultimately getting you in the right mindset to achieving and living the life that you truly deserve.

> *Life is full of little choices. There is an old saying: "What is popular is not always right; what is right is not always popular." We don't always make the right choices or do the right things. Mistakes are a normal part of living and to be expected. All people make mistakes; it's part of living. When we make a mistake, we gain more self-awareness and, hopefully, learn a life's lesson. It's True! We can learn by our mistakes. What is more important, we can avoid some mistakes if we take the time to identify our personal values and ethics.*

CHAPTER 1

Research

Whilst developing Urlaw™, we realised that the real value was acknowledging that we didn't need to come up with the most profound solution, that does this stuff, and smoke and fire comes out the top, and it whizzes and bangs, we knew we didn't need to do that, we basically created a sound simple, straightforward system giving structure that is going to change things for people through 'The Law of Attraction'.

So when we were looking at our model and philosophy, some of it seemed pretty straightforward stuff, some of it seemed to be really basic, sometimes it felt so basic that we couldn't base the model on the simple points, but we actually could. I have read through countless people's reviews that have said, "It's not told me this, and it has not told me that!" and the simple answer to that is, it is because it's not supposed to! That's not what it's here for, which changed how we thought about what my role was and what I was doing. We realised I'm clearly and simply trying to make sure people understand what it is that they've got in their hands and how to use it. It literally is as simple as that, we're showing you what we've got, and we're showing you how to use it.

Overall our aim is to make the whole concept of The Law of Attraction easier to digest, much more consumable, much easier to work with, helping people to think of it in a simple way. There is a difference between simple and simplistic, the concept behind this is not actually simplistic, but what I am doing is making it simple so that people can understand and digest it. When we went through it, we found specific gaps, and we addressed them by coming up with our own answers to them. We went through 100 plus reviews, and each of them had over 10 comments and 100's of different responses which allowed us to pick up all the different problems. We charted them into a sheet understanding what problems people were facing, we ended up with a number of different problems, and then we categorised them into different areas, I also did some additional research and amongst the 1000's of people who also did go through 'The Secret', I went through and pulled where people felt unsatisfied, understood where they felt they weren't getting traction, where they felt that this had let them down, and I have included the responses to each of those problems as well.

So when we sat down and really dug in there, we found there were some really constant problems, so we furthered our research which I also put my own personal experiences to that research, amongst friends and colleagues and what was really interesting was going into a lot of the online spaces, the communities and especially places like Amazon, where you can read reviews, and we got a real understanding of the positive and negative feedback to The Law of Attraction.

What we found was a percentage of people that straight don't believe it, it was just under half, 33% of people just struggled with the whole concept; that's not who we are really trying to help out here, because I think if you are at a point where you just don't believe something, you will find a different solution to help you out in life. What we found for the other 70% there were some very specific problem areas, some of the first areas people struggled with was actually putting it all into practice, they found it was a great concept, they felt energised, but when putting into practice, kind of run out of steam, which leads to the next problem which is strategy, they didn't feel they were left with an actual overall road map, no step by step; people don't really know where they are going, there was no order in which to do things, and when we talk about an order to do things, they even felt the things they needed to do, the actual tactics; they weren't too detailed, they were left with this feeling of not really knowing what to do next or what items to even take to try and do next.

There was an interesting one, about 3% mentioned that it created an element of fear within them, and that fear was related to feeling of out of control like things were not in their hands, that this Law of Attraction had defined everything that happened in their past, but we have some interesting information around that, that we will share with you shortly that is around our foundation model and in our foundation model we do a lot to help you to be able to understand what it actually is, what it's not and what it takes.

The final problem people which around 6% were struggling with was being able to see proof of quantifiable results of success in application of the Law of Attraction, so there are some of the problems that we understand, hopefully there's something in there that you have been able to see, relate to and understand and were able to see and relate to.

We also found that most people divert another without finding out what the root cause is - Going Metta as such, an example to this is, us going to the doctor and saying to the doctor "I've got a sore throat" and the doctor not trying to find out why you potentially have a sore throat, and just saying "oh you have a sore throat, here just take this!" Most would say "If you don't like this, read that, just literally shipping you off without finding out the root cause. So we wanted to really understand and furthered our research to people who had read the follow-up books to 'The Secret' discovering that out of 100, 40% felt like it was just the same information repeated.

We asked ourselves, what did the original (The Secret) not give? What did it not give that people were so narked about if you will? What fundamental reasons are people disappointed with? Was it the fact that people are coming to it for a different purpose? We understood one of the main reasons why people are not getting what they want from it because you have to know what it is, what it's not and what it takes and we believe knowing those three things will completely change what anyone will expect from it! (We will expand on this later) If someone goes into it thinking it's the sole life for them, it's going to make you obsolete of making decisions, and things are just going to happen, then you will be mistaken. We believe it is worth clarifying that immediately, that's not going to happen.

We went on 2 different management courses, and until they said this is how you run a project you wouldn't necessarily know that's how you would structure a company, I mean it's obvious as soon as someone says it, it's blatantly obvious and everyone thinks, well, why didn't I think of that? Because it isn't that obvious. For example, when you get in a car, and you're learning how to drive, the whole clutch shifting thing it's like what! And you're being told put the clutch in first and then you hear a screech, then it's like, No, put the clutch down first, then put it in first gear, then you stall the car then you try again, and it's explained, why you need to put the clutch down first, because you need to disengage the clutch and the engine to allow you to put it in gear and let the gearbox connect back up to gear, it's obvious now when you start to drive, you put the clutch down first, obviously you would put the clutch down first but it isn't obvious until somebody explains to you why you're doing it that way round. A Lot of people learn how to drive and never know why they are putting the clutch down first; they just get told that's what they need to do and they do it.

This is what I am saying about the information out there, we had to question it at a very specific level because some of the words that we use and the phrases that we will use, were very carefully constructed, because we realised when people hear things like, 'Every Positive and Every Negative Event that happened with you was attracted to you, by you, this statement has created confusion and mess, we are going to make it nice and clear and simple. There are obviously things that are out of your control. There is a phrase - "Every Cloud has a Silver Lining' What that doesn't mean is that the cloud is no longer a cloud - it's still a cloud, situations can be bad, "we can take something that is beneficial out of a bad situation", and the most common phrase is - You have got to take the positive out of it! Which we believe can be insulting, there are scenarios that are just not positive like a mother watching her children being blown up in war, there is nothing positive about that situation! The instant brushing off of stuff is what people struggle with in terms of accepting how to get this moved on. We felt if a more pragmatic way came out then people won't feel so bad about taking on the rest of the information, you can't just knock stuff straight off, this isn't about not acknowledging things that are negative or bad, it's a tool for working out how to deal with them, it's not a blanket that gets thrown on top of stuff and gets covered away and put to the side.

The Law of Attraction can work so much easier for you if you are able to stick to a system, so I'm not saying, this does or doesn't work, I am saying, this can all work a lot easier if you know how to work it. The Law of Attraction does a great thing for people; it will always deliver what you are thinking and what you are feeling. It works in each moment; it doesn't care about your past, it works in the present. As mentioned earlier we found that people are struggling to be able to get it and to make it work for them. So the important thing is, if you know how to work with it then you will get results.

I realised one of the big problems with The Law of Attraction is:

1. People aren't necessarily completely clear on what they're getting
2. They're not clear on what they're not getting
3. They're not clear on what it takes to make it work with them.

Through my own experiences of applying the Law of Attraction, I realised I was dealing with the 6 specific problems when trying to apply it and there was only really 6 principles that I needed to focus on to be able to make it really work in my favour in all aspects of my life. I now have a way of making it work, using this tool will get you almost anything you want, and we're going to move on and show you how you can get around all of these things.

We're going to open up this whole theory by saying, there's a foundation you first have to understand, which consists of 3 things that actually make up the foundation elements, they're not about what you have got to do, they're about what you need to understand. I'm going to go into the first part with the key understandings that you must have, which will release you into being able to do more or get more. We can't even get into how you can apply the Law of Attraction before we make sure you're totally cool and clear about what to do. If we are successful at doing that, I think from the research that I have been doing, and my personal experiences, it's going to give back something quite useful.

> *It's unlimited what the universe can bring when you understand the great secret that thoughts become things*

The entire concept of the Law of Attraction can be summed up in just three words. **Like attracts like**. Positively focusing your thoughts on the things you want in your life, will allow those things to come into your life. Your thoughts and emotions emit vibrational energy that attracts that which you are giving the most attention to.

The power of the human brain is not yet fully understood, but that doesn't mean you can't harness it to discover your true potential, creating a whole new life for yourself starting right now. You will also be able to share your findings with others to produce powerful changes in their lives as well!

> *"Research is to see what everybody else has seen and to think what nobody else has thought"* Albert Szent-Gyorgyi

CHAPTER 2

What it is, What it's not and What it takes

The first thing you need to understand and be very clear on is what it is in terms of how it works, which consists of the three elements that we just spoke about. We are breaking it down in terms of What it is, What it's not and What it takes to make it work with you and for you, so let's get started with the foundation, we need to really understand exactly what the Law of Attraction is.

Simply put, the Law of Attraction is the ability to attract into our lives whatever we are focusing on. It is believed that regardless of age, nationality or religious belief, we are all susceptible to the laws which govern the Universe, including the Law of Attraction. It is the Law of Attraction which uses the power of the mind to translate whatever is in our thoughts and materialise them into reality. In basic terms, **thoughts turn into things, the more we focus on things, the quicker they become our reality!** How we feel also plays a big part in this, as we have an emotional response to our thoughts, this is why it is so important to be aware of the way we are feeling as our thoughts will reflect our emotions.

WHAT IT IS

It is a very powerful tool to be able to Implement and Manage Change in all areas of your life when you work with it and not against it, that's what it actually is. It certainly leads to an Increased Level of Awareness and the more mindful we are, the more aware we are, and the more we can achieve. In terms of understanding what it is, a lot of people feel that it applies to everything and I will make a subtle change to that description, the Law of Attraction can be applied to anything, but it is not the results of everything. Is it going to change everything? No, but could it change anything? Absolutely - There is hardly anything that impacts everything. However, some things could impact anything; we have to keep in mind that there are other impacts in play, which leads us into what it's not.

WHAT IT'S NOT

It is not the only Law in application, it is only one of the universal laws, there are other Laws in play, and it's not isolated to being the only Law that can work at any point in time, there's the Law of Cause and Effect, there are other Laws like The Law Gravity, it's not like you just think to yourself, "I'm not into Gravity being applied to me", and you become exempt from gravity, it is what it is! Regardless of age, nationality or religious belief, we are all susceptible to the laws which govern the Universe, including the Law of Attraction.

The Law of Attraction is not a badness blocker, it's not a Mosquito Repellent, you can't get a bottle of Urlaw™ give it a little shake and spray it all over yourself and just protect yourself, then ping the badness just drops off, or you become invincible from everything bad, that's not what it is. Things happen in life; it's just the way the cookie crumbles! It doesn't keep you alive or stop you passing away; this isn't going to stop your loved ones being left from you, there is the natural cycle of life, things are going to happen. This isn't about, not acknowledging things that are negative and bad, it's a tool for working out how to deal with them, and it's not a blanket that gets thrown on top of stuff and gets covered away and put to the side.

The second thing, It's not going to give you your Morals, and it's not going to give you your Principles, it will help you be more resolute with the Morals, Principles, and Values you have or inspiring to have. It is certainly not an excuse for us to evade the human function, of having Morals, Principles, and Values, we need these in place for this to work. If you are married and desired a tall dark and handsome man that is not your husband and a week later you attract and meet a tall dark and handsome man, it doesn't mean you can commit adultery! Which leads us to the last point; It's not actually a guidebook to life or how to do things, that will get you to what you want, that's down to you to work out which steps to take next and it is definitely not a one-stop solution, this is not going to tell you what your desires are, therefore you need to work out yourself, So the final thing we need to understand is what it takes.

WHAT IT TAKES

It most certainly takes an **open mind**, a **Positive Mental Attitude**, It takes, a *change of perception*, not looking at what's going wrong, but ***what's going right***, knowing you have the power to influence and if you go out and give the best of what you've got, it's more likely that you will accomplish what you set out to accomplish. It takes a *tremendous amount of focus* on the things you're aiming to achieve, without focus this won't work, and in order to accomplish something incredible, something remarkable, it takes ***immense focus***, it takes large commitment and you most definitely need to be **tenacious**, because as we know, all the greatest things take time to materialise, with a good structure, a solid plan and detailed set of action steps, this is entirely reachable, and when you do, the results are unbelievably rich and outstanding.

It takes a great deal of **patience**, as without patience you will find that you won't trust the process, It takes a *high level of Appreciation* and last, but not least it takes community, meaning your environment dictates your performance, so if everyone around you is negative, you are more likely to be the same and vice versa!

> *"The secret of change is to focus all of your energy, not on fighting the old, but on building the new."*
>
> *When attitude is changed, thought is changed*
>
> *When thought is changed, behaviour is changed*
>
> *When behaviour is changed, action is changed*
>
> *When action is changed, result is changed*

CHAPTER 3

Step 1 - Define

What You Need To Know:

This is the beginning of a mind training process, so actually, we have to create a strong structure just like building a wall, defining it one brick at a time to get the results we set out to achieve. By doing this with your mind, you actually become much stronger at being able to hold your focus on a new and particular way of thinking. Finding new things to focus on will help with letting go of the minute things that do not serve you in any way shape or form; however, they have your attention because you are yet to define exactly what you want.

Things seem to be Spoken of as if they just happened, and you just miraculously get this paradigm shift in your thinking because you heard about the law of attraction, and everything that has 'gone wrong' in your life just gets forgotten about, well it doesn't!

The first thing is being able to be decisive about what you want to accomplish and achieve in this life, and until you are aware and gain clarity of these things, you will find yourself going round in circles, day after day, year after year with maybe different faces and different places however the same as always! Leading us to **Self-Awareness.**

When you typically see things in a negative light, you can actually struggle to think about the things you are good at and vice versa leading to your emotional state to be on a high or a low. Self-Awareness requires an understanding of you, including your strengths and your weaknesses and then choosing which path you actually want to go down. Self-awareness isn't just about focusing on your emotions it is also about focusing on your strengths, it's about accepting your faults and failures, becoming at peace with yourself, your flaws and your capabilities. What one person is good at does not mean that you will also be good at, however that does not mean you are a failure; it just simply means we all have different strengths and weaknesses.

One of the biggest things that most successful people seem to do is have a target, they don't roughly aim somewhere, they're very precise about what they are aiming for and most of the time, people are quite definitive about it, so being able to sit down and define where you want to go, is a great place to start, it's a positive location to be and is the start of getting what you want.

They say if you do what you have always done you will always get what you have always got - We say "*If you always think what you used to think, you will only ever achieve what you used to accomplish.*"

"Your attitude NOT your aptitude will determine your Altitude" - Zig Ziglar

This is also about accountability realising that you are in control of what happens next and that you always have been influential in what happens to you. Accepting that the past could have been influenced, will allow bigger things to be accomplished - like leaving the past firmly behind before stepping into a new world of positivity, (*Positivity - Frequent experience of present emotions-*

Frequently having joy, hope, gratitude, pride, amusement and Inspiration) as if you continue to hold on to negative experiences of the past, this will keep you living your past!

> *"Accept your past without regrets, handle your present with confidence, and face your future with no fear."* - Unknown

From the beginning of this process, you need be prepared to drop all excuses for why something can't be done and be prepared to find reasons to **why it can be done**. If you walk around thinking whatever you want, rather than being particular about what you are thinking, then you will end up getting whatever turns up, probably not what you were dreaming about. This is about becoming ultra-aware of yourself, your thoughts, your actions, your words, your energy and being Accountable for the way you THINK, FEEL, ACT and SPEAK!

> *"I call the mind a parachute, as it only works well when it's open, and that's the way people have to be, they have to be open to suggestions, open to listening to someone who has achieved"* - Tom Hopkins

To be able to be successful in implementing The Secret, as we mentioned one of the secrets is Tenacity - This is bigger than being persistent, this is a change in the way you generally think, it is not just being persistent about that one thing, it's about being tenacious generally. That starts with the way we conceptualise things in our minds, it is deeper going into, making sure you have a very clear solid concept; of what it is you are trying to move to so that you can stick to it because if you have a loose picture in your mind then you have no reason to stay grounded in moving towards it - don't give up mentally. This is not about how good you are; it's how positive you are towards getting things done, which is going to be the definition of how high you are going to fly!

The most common mistake people make when trying to incorporate the Law of Attraction techniques into their life is allowing that destructive negative energy to dominate their minds. There is a very simple and straightforward solution for overcoming even the most stubborn and dominant negativity. All you have to do is remember to be **N.I.C.E.**! What happens when you are being **N.I.C.E.**? Nice things happen! I'm Sharing this easy to remember method with you, and you will be able to harness the true power of positive energy as well.

Here's what we mean by this.

> *Notice when your thoughts and energy take on a negative vibe.*
>
> *Intervene by telling negativity to get lost and realize what kind of person it makes you.*
>
> *Change your way of thinking using positive affirmations and other positive activities.*
>
> *Embrace the way positive energy makes you feel.*

As we mentioned earlier, having a clear target of what you are going for is one of the most important aspects of being able to focus your mind. Being clear about what you want and why you want it is crucial to getting what you want. Taking that time out for yourself and working on you is extremely important, to define exactly what you want out of life; asking yourself questions like, What am I looking to achieve or what am I looking to accomplish is crucial.

"I have looked in the mirror every morning and asked myself if today were the last day of my life would I want to do what I am about to do today, whenever the answer has been no, for too many times in a row, I know I need to change something. Remembering that I'll be dead soon is the most important tool I have ever encountered to help me make the big choices in life, because almost everything, internal expectation, all pride, all fear of embarrassment or failure, these things just fall away in the face of death, leaving only what is truly important. Remembering that you are going to die is the best way that I know to avoid the trap of thinking you have something to lose, you are already naked, and there is no reason not to follow your heart.

Your time is limited so don't waste it living someone else's life, don't be trapped by dogma with living with results of someone else is thinking, don't let the noise of other's opinions drown out your inner voice and importance, have the courage to follow your heart and intuition; they somehow already know what you truly want to become, everything else is somebody." - Steve Jobs

Again, when trying to apply the secret there is a heavy amount of it which focuses on the mind, so being able to clear the mind allows you to have a lot more control of all the next steps including Self-Awareness and putting things in compartmentalising things- This is a big piece of applying it because you need to be able to control your mind, we talk about all the different parts to controlling your mind, part of that is emptying process at the beginning, you have got to be able to clear it. If you can't clear space to be able to take on a new way of thinking, you are going to struggle, so the best way to be able to get to a clear state of mind is to meditate. It's a simple act of sitting in silence for 10-15 minutes on a daily basis focusing one's mind allowing the answers to questions and problems which are all found within ourselves! (Please do your own research).

When I have said to people, "if you focus on the thing that you want"... and people often mistake that with, if you think about the things you want, you will have them, you've got to focus on them (to direct one's attention or efforts) you have to take time to plan them, you've got to physically take action towards them, what I am saying is, this isn't just a Thinkathon, although having clear forward thinking thoughts about what you want is absolutely necessary, there is action to be taken whilst thinking. However, it's that alignment of your thoughts and actions in the things that you want that helps towards the accomplishment of them.

So to put this in context, first of all you need to spend time thinking about what you even want to do, if you are not clear on what you are trying to do, you will not get there, If you can list all of those things, you're going to have a really good perspective of what you need to do now to help some of the other things happen. Could you imagine, you and a friend decide to go out for a coffee and decide on taking separate cars, and you said to your friend, "Right, I'll see you there, Wait! Where shall I meet you? Don't worry I'll see you there!

If you don't define the name of the coffee shop and its exact location you are meeting at, then what're the chances that you will end up at the same place? You were both thinking 'coffee' however unless defined in location; you are very likely to end up at different coffee shops. Or could you imagine If you were travelling from London to Scotland using a Sat Nav, and you said to the Sat Nav "Take me to Scotland" You would have to enter a Postcode or an actual location otherwise the Sat Nav would guide you to anywhere in Scotland, and it probably won't be the place you wanted to go. Do you see the importance of defining and being clear on what you're doing and where you're going? On that note, have you heard the saying, failing to plan, is planning to fail? Have you ever gone shopping without a shopping list? If yes, then you will know that most times when you have done that, you will come home with everything other than what you actually wanted as failing to plan, is planning to fail! Getting into the habit of defining and planning is part of this process.

> *"The journey of a thousand miles always begins with one step"* - LAO-TZU

If a business come to us and said "It's the start of a new year and by the end of this year, we want to be at 3 quarters of a million turnover", we then say, Taking your products, how many of these products would you need to do, to be able to produce 3 quarters of a million turnover? And then they would they go 'Oh, we need to do 73 extra' 'Great! What would you need to do, to produce 73 of those?" Well, we would need to do 3 times the amount of this. Now they know to do 3 quarters of a million, they would need to produce 3x the amount of sales marketing volume, whereas before they were just thinking "I wish we had 3 quarters of a million!" so effectively the same example applies.

> *"If you don't design your own life plan, chances are you'll fall into someone else's plan. And guess what they have planned for you? Not much"* - Jim Rohn

What we are saying is, what result would you want to have in a week's time? Have you seriously thought about how you would get to get that result in 7 days? And as it happens, there are things that you want to happen in 4 weeks' time. What would you need to do now, to get there by the end of the month? There is no point somebody saying "I want to lose 3lbs by the end of the day" Well, you needed to start that process a week ago not today!

> *"Most people overestimate what they can do in a year, and they underestimate what they can do in two or three decades."* -Tony Robbins

What You Need To Do - Actions:

Getting a fresh notepad to specifically define and write down what you want, by listing in order of how soon you would like or need them to happen is a great place to start.

Why would we be asking you to write it down? Through research, we found people who commit their thoughts to paper have a significantly higher success rate of achieving the things they have written down. It's to do with how our neurons work in our body, that if we actually go through the handwriting process and write things down it actually re communicates it back to our brain the relevance and importance of it. If you write things down, you have almost made a commitment to it. If you write something down on a 'to do' list, you're pretty committed to making it happen.

Examples and Analogies:

If someone is going to build a brick wall, they need to know the direction the wall is going before they start laying the bricks down and building it. Just slapping bricks down and thinking you're going to get the brick wall you want at the end is not the answer, as what you will have is a line of bricks that might not lead to the way you intended, maybe that's how they ended up making the great wall of China!

Next, you will find exercises that we have set out for you to fill in, helping you to get started with the Urlaw™ System. We suggest you start with a short-term list, like, what you would like as soon as the next day and we're not just talking about physical stuff this includes emotional states, you may want to feel emotions of satisfaction, love, peace, harmony, unless you clearly state these emotions, then you're less likely to be aware what state of emotions you are feeling.

We have provided space at the end of this chapter in order for you to answer the following.

1. What is vital that you feel you would want or need to happen in the next 7 days?

2. Once you have answered the above you can then make a list of everything you would like to happen/experience within the next 4 weeks, then double that time to 2 months and if you can, then think to double that, so it's half a year and then think to double that to a year.

3. Actually, break this down. We only want you to focus on what's immediately important to you right now and what is realistic to be able to happen immediately so if you want to learn to drive a car and obtain a driver's license tomorrow but have never driven a car before, then realistically, it's not going to happen as soon as tomorrow! Ask yourself what is most important to you? What do you want today and tomorrow? Remember, having a clear target of what you are going for is one of the most important aspects of being able to focus your mind. Being clear about what you want is crucial to getting what you want.

Always be very clear, as unclear thoughts will result in unclear results.

Many people will say they want financial wealth, but they haven't taken the time out to define, visualise and understand how to obtain financial wealth, and what living that lifestyle means.

Financial Wealth - As stated in the book "Rich Dad Poor Dad' by Robert Kiyosaki, Wealth is how long you can go on living your existing lifestyle if you stopped working today. It's the number of days you can continue living the same as you do without doing anything different.

Someone very wealthy can stop what they are doing and carry on exactly as they are for years and years and ultimately ask themselves "how much could I give to my entire group of important people" - the mega-wealthy could support a large number of people and still not have to work. They could probably sustain so many people's lifestyle out of their wealth.

How wealthy someone wants to be is different, some people want a different lifestyle and want to be wealthy in that lifestyle. There are different levels of it if you are prepared to write down what your daily life is like if you want gourmet food and having people wait on you every day, it's going to take a little longer depending on your current beliefs and current lifestyle.

Most people if they carried on living the way they live now and they stopped working, within a number of days they wouldn't be able to sustain their lifestyle. So if you want to be able to make a difference and live financial wealth then define it. If you are generally saying things like "I want more money," and you haven't specified the amount you want, and you receive an extra £5, then you actually achieved your outcome. You weren't specific with your outcome however you did receive more money! Think in terms of outcomes and remember ***Clarity is power!***

We're pushing for definition, so these things can be much clearer and much stronger in you when going for what you want. Define what you want to accomplish in these stages, we have provided extra pages at the back of this book in order for you to continue writing if you run out of space and for notes purposes.

What Doing Define Looks Like - Exercises:

1. **Within the next day**

_____
_____
_____
_____
_____
_____

2. **Within the next week**

_____
_____
_____
_____
_____
_____

Now that you have got the immediate things out of your mind, and have practiced and got some great results, we can take a moment and focus on a slightly bigger picture, not a massive one but if you had to think about, what you wanted to accomplish in a month, what would be included that you haven't already covered in what you are going to accomplish this week.

3. *Within the next 4 weeks*

_____
_____
_____
_____
_____

4. *Within the next 3 months*

_____
_____
_____
_____
_____
_____

5. *Within the next 6 months*

_____
_____
_____
_____
_____
_____

6. *Within the next 12 months*

_____
_____
_____
_____
_____
_____

So now you have a list that radiates from immediate wants, desires and needs all the way out to things that could happen in the next 3 to 6 to 12 months. Now you know exactly what you want and your period behind it. You can look at them with clarity and say, right these are all of my targets that I only really need to be focused on in the short term, then all your energies can go into making those things happen that are most important to you on your list for now.

We recommend you look at your list on a daily basis, make it part of your daily routine after brushing your teeth when you awaken in the morning and before you go to sleep at night, maybe pin it up on your ceiling so you don't lose focus, reminding yourself why you have chosen to achieve the things on your list, helping you to continue moving towards them even when you are faced with obstacles. Most things will be presented with some kind of obstacle, and it is up to you climb over them, and I am sure you have heard at some point in your life; practice makes perfect. Never give up!

> *"You're only going to yield what you focus on"* - Urlaw™
>
> *"Progress is impossible without change, and those who cannot change their minds cannot change anything."* – George Bernard Shaw

CHAPTER 4

Step 2 - Demand

What you Need to Know:

Step 2 of the Urlaw™ System is Demand and Demand is all about demanding in detail, demanding with that makes it significantly more realistic. Here we are talking about everything that you are capable of doing and actually having that agreement with yourself, by actually asking yourself permission to be able to go ahead and do the things you want to do. So what we are saying is the more detail the request, the more likely you are going to take yourself seriously and work towards making it happen and convincing yourself along the way that you are going to make it. The more detail you request from yourself, the better, so this is all about asking yourself more questions, and really getting into the details of what it is you are wanting, and when we say detail we also mean visual detail, see yourself doing it, visualise it. It's really about getting deep into the details.

One of the reasons we are saying to go into detail is because, if you care to dream it out, you may realise that you are focusing on something you don't actually want. So you need to be crystal clear, just to clarify further another example of focusing on something that you don't actually want, but thought you wanted is, someone we actually worked with before, and they thought they wanted to have a business that Sold lots of products from a warehouse and what they had said was...

To be happy and what would make them happy is, if they sold more of the stuff that they already sold, and then they would be very happy, but when we started asking them details, like, why do you want that? Is that going to bring you happiness? What's the reason why you want a warehouse? They said they'll have a lot more money and they felt they would have more freedom. However, we pointed out, that they won't have more freedom because they will be tied to a warehouse which has got all of their stuff in it. We explained that in order to have a warehouse they would then have to hire security guards 24/7, along with CCTV, etc. We continued to dig in and asked, what made them feel really good? Whilst giving them consultation and advice, we realised it was a completely different thing that they wanted, and pointed out that it was a consultancy business that they actually wanted. Far from where we started right!? Can you imagine if we just worked towards the first thing they had asked for without breaking it down, they would have ended up with a great big warehouse, full of stock, that they would have been worrying about and couldn't leave unattended, creating worry and less freedom, exactly the opposite of what they stated they wanted!

> *"Goals become like magnets, they pull you in that direction, and the better you describe them, the more they pull"* - Jim Rohn

So if you want happiness then Happiness in itself as a definition is literally a state of being happy, this is why it is so hard for people to define it because it's a fleeting emotion. You'll have it, and at some point, the accusation of something is what makes somebody happy. So if happiness is a state of being, and most people feel it when they acquire something, wouldn't it be a good idea to feel happy regardless of what you acquire? How about learn from yourself, by asking yourself what makes you feel happiness, once you know that very important detail about yourself then do things that helps you stay in that state of happiness, because it's not the things that make you happy, it's the choices you make in life that helps the happiness shine through you and then you don't have to rely on things, experiences or situations to help you feel happy.

> *"The things that you think make you happy is not the actual thing; it's the journey you take to acquire the things you want"* - *Urlaw*™

If you want to go and see a certain country, instead of just saying, "I would love to go to Spain, or I would love to go to Italy" If you never make it deeper than that, then you are lessening the chance of going right? If you said, "I would love to go to the Bastogne in Belgium, I would love to see the Leaning Tower of Pisa, I would love to have an espresso sitting outside the Bastogne, I would love to try Parmesan Cheese in Florence, the fact that you're now going into detail, is going to fuel the demand process, so make the demand in more detailed, don't just ask for it, make the request to yourself more detailed, ask yourself what you would really want out of those things, push yourself to be able to say, "I want a car," ask about the specification and why that particular specification, make your vision very detailed.

As we were just saying, there is a separation between someone saying "I wouldn't mind doing that or I wouldn't mind doing this" but if you take it one step further in your mind, you will actually be able to say to yourself, "you know what, I actually do want to do this, and I would like to do this," and you are pretty much self-requesting, you're making a formal request back into your own mind, confirming this isn't a dream, this isn't 'Pie in the sky'. When people are demanding things, they usually don't just demand it and that's it, they tend to give a full justification to why they want it especially children!

Examples and Analogies:

If you've got a child, and they say "I want a PlayStation 4", they won't just say "I want a PlayStation!" they will continue to say "I really want it, and you may reply "well, you'll have to be good!" and then they move into demand mode and they will show you how much they want it. They say "Please, you know that game you gave me, well the last 2 only come out on PlayStation 4 and I love that game, it's my favourite, and all my friends have it and if I don't have it, I won't be able to play with all my friends" They will give you all of the reasons to why they want it. When people are demanding things they usually don't just demand it and that's it, they give full justification to why that thing is, but sometimes in the middle of that process, you kind of find out that what you thought you want, you kinda don't want (probably not likely to happen in the example just given above).

As we mentioned earlier in the example of the business owner. The other reason you need to focus on your demands more clearly is to make sure whatever you think you have decided that you want is actually really the thing that you want and you've got all of the good reasons, the benefits and the pros. Demanding something means we need to demand more information about it and more information about why we want it, demanding yourself to know why demanding you to ask why and then demand that it happens! Once you have clarified this to yourself, you will start building the confidence to move forward.

The Owner of Vercov Consulting gave this great example of not demanding that we both agreed would be great to share; he said, "I always wanted to have my own business, when I was a kid, I would be drawing little company logos with my own name in it. When at college, me and my friend would joke about it saying 'Marcus Macarthy' the fact that we joked about it said it was clearly something we wanted to do, what we didn't do, is request it, we didn't demand that that happens because what we would have done as soon as we left college is, we would have done it! But we didn't turn it into something tangible and real because we didn't ask ourselves to accomplish it, so we both went off to work for other people, but at some point in that journey, I decided to ask myself and define what I wanted, and I said I don't want to work for someone else anymore and do you know what? I would like to work for myself, that's what I would really like to do, I would love to do that please (he is self-requesting here) Now I'm starting to take myself seriously and saying well you kinda have to look into that Andre.

It's that Alter Ego, were saying listen, just letting you know, I would really love to do this, subconscious answers back, well how much do you want it? And you're like, well, I really want to do it, well, what would it look like if you're serious about doing it? I don't know if you're serious, how do I know, if you're serious? You say, listen, If I run my own business, it would be really different, I would make it, so people have flexibility in my workforce, I would want them to work from anywhere I would have a reward system, it's never been a better time to do this and so forth, you would go into detail and now you're really asking! We're not saying just ask the top level questions; we're saying the moment you start demanding the details is the moment you will start thinking about it in a more detailed way the more likely you are going to take yourself seriously and work towards making it happen!

What You Need To Do - Actions:

There are key questions you need to ask yourself about everything you have decided that you want, short term and long term. Having that perspective will give you a lot more conviction about the choices that you have made and it will help you believe in your choices when you make it rich, detailed, populated and structured.

So in step one, you defined what you want, and now in step 2, it's time to go through your list and demand the details of what you have defined to find out if it's really what you want.

You will also need to be clear and specific to 'WHY' you want what you want.

What are your reasons for wanting it? What is your purpose for wanting it? Answer this with emotion. The why's is what drives us, if you want to buy a house, then why do you want to buy it? What will it do for you? How will you feel when you buy it?

This is very powerful and effective as once you write it and state your reasons 'WHY' you want it, then you can always read it to fuel your emotional drive to your outcome, especially to help you bypass any obstacles that may appear along with your journey to getting what you want.

80% of success is Why and 20% is How. Know your reasons why!

We've written what we want and now the next Key questions to ask yourself when demanding details in regards to everything you have decided that you want, short term and long term are as follows:

What Doing Demand Looks Like - Exercise

1. *Why do I want it?*

   _____
   _____
   _____
   _____
   _____
   _____

2. *What's going to be different if I have it?*

   _____
   _____
   _____
   _____
   _____
   _____

3. *What benefits will it give me?*

   _____
   _____
   _____
   _____
   _____
   _____

4. *How will it enrich my life?*

_____
_____
_____
_____
_____

5. *How will it help me to help others?*

_____
_____
_____
_____
_____

6. *What other reasons do I want it for?*

_____
_____
_____
_____
_____

7. *What will it feel like if I have it?*

_____
_____
_____
_____
_____

8. *What would it look like if I did have it?*

_____
_____
_____
_____
_____
_____

9. *What would I change once I've got it?*

_____
_____
_____
_____
_____
_____

10. *What would I get rid of once I've got it?*

_____
_____
_____
_____
_____
_____

> *"Wanting something is not enough. You must hunger for it. Your motivation must be absolutely compelling in order to overcome the obstacles that will invariably come your way"* - Les Brown

CHAPTER 5

Step 3 - Commit

What You Need To Know:

Now you have completed step one and step two, it is time to learn how to commit and we believe, commitment is that turning point in your life when you seize the moment and convert it into an opportunity to change your destiny. This whole section is about learning the meaning of commitment. Firstly, we suggest you become committed to implementing and managing change, to do this, you must be open-minded, and following all 6 principles will in time lead to that increased level of awareness, and as we mentioned, the more mindful we are, the more we can achieve.

Through research, we found there are 3 main reasons people quit.

1. *People who have a history of failing at getting what they want.*
2. *Perfectionists*
3. *Lack of faith*

Each of them is related to each other, so obviously the more you fail, the less committed you're going to be and the less committed you are, the more likely you're going to fail. If you're less committed you're not going to believe in it as much so technically speaking, you've got less faith (we consider faith to be a combination of belief, trust and confidence, this will be explained later) and if you haven't got faith then you are more likely to doubt yourself and not pursue what you want; basically it's in this sort of Perpetua's cycle. There is a system of failure and not committing to things basically means you get into this cycle of not getting what you want.

Be aware of being in perfection mode and go against it, do it even if it's not perfect, go against lack of faith and boost your faith and fight against the history of failure; things repeating themselves and commit to getting what you want. Your involvement in getting what you want is actually significant; you can't list it, dream it, think of it and only partially contribute to getting it. You've got to be wholly committed, singularly focused; irrespective of the hurdles, and there will be hurdles and in some cases, the hurdles may appear to be impossible to overcome, however with every problem there is a solution, so you have identified the problem and once you have figured out the solution then only focus on the solution, and there is hardly anything that is impossible, the word itself spells **I'M POSSIBLE!**

> *"The difference between impossible and possible lies in a person's determination"* - Tommy Lasorda

We believe integrity *(Integrity - The quality of being honest and having strong moral principles)* plays a big part in commitment. If you say you're going to do something, you need to do it! The reason is not that you told someone else you'll do it, it's because you said it, so you should do it, and feel accountable for your words. The biggest test of integrity is what you would do if no-one else knew if no-one else was there, would you still do it?

This is ultimately about actually building the foundation layers of being true to yourself, being a more solid individual because solid people who are true to themselves tend to actually get what they want. Being true to yourself is what it is.

This is something that you will be learning to do from yourself to yourself, by yourself and for yourself. So it's from you, by you, to you and for you.

"Either you run the day or the day runs you" - Jim Rohn

If there is ever a time to be the positive context of selfish, this is it. This is the appropriate and correct way to be selfish, not the other nasty way; this is the time you need to apply to yourself. Most people who fail at reaching their dreams fail not from lack of ability but from lack of commitment.

"Whilst we are sitting here working out whether we are committed to something or not, someone is out there actually going and getting the things you wish to have" - Urlaw™

What You Need To Do (Actions)

Having faith in yourself - In relation to commitment having faith is a very big thing, many almost brush it off to fast, and to light, so you have got to have faith in yourself. Someone can believe in someone and not trust them, you can believe that someone didn't do something, but you can not necessarily trust that they won't do it in the future, you might not have confidence that they wouldn't do something in the future, but if you have faith in someone, clearly you trust them, you believe in them, and you have confidence in them. So flipping this back over to yourself means, that you have got to trust you, you've got to believe you and have the confidence in you to be able to get there which means that there are some other ingredients to becoming committed.

> *"Faith is like Wifi, it's invisible, but it has the power to connect you to what you need"* - Unknown

We thought a good way to look at commitment is like a cake and to make a cake you have to have the right ingredients. So we're going to breakdown commitment like it's a cake

So let's look at this like it's a big round cake, there's a couple of key elements at the beginning by having trust, belief and confidence in yourself; actually there is also a couple of extra ingredients that get thrown in there, not necessarily in gigantic quantities but without them you're not going to get the same result, there's got to be an honesty about realistically how much is required. Some people commit to something that they think is going to be easy and when they realise it's not, they give up.

Let your faith be bigger than your fears

To commit to something underlies the fact that you have some idea of how hard it's going to be, you don't have to commit to something that's easy, I guess it means we won't mentally downplay the challenge that's gonna be presented because that's committing to something different.

Examples and Analogies:

An Olympian commits way before they have any idea of the results that they might get 4 years before, maybe even longer before they choose to commit to being a part of the Olympic Games. 5 years ago, after the last Olympics, a group of individuals decided that they will be competing in Rio 2016 and they are going to go for medals. They looked into it, they saw it was going to take unbelievable training, they understood that they were going to have to eat differently, that they are going to have to do what their friends are not doing and they have to be prepared to do that for four years straight! After knowing what it would take and the time scale, they committed to taking part. Every one of those challengers whether they win this time or not, they were fully committed to training for the Olympics in 2016 anyone who didn't commit to winning the Olympics had to go, they want to be in the 2020 games, they must have committed a couple of years ago, otherwise they're not going to win, they might not even get there. If you commit, there's a chance to take Gold, Silver or Bronze. You could even get yourself to such a committed level, that you become the best in your country, first you've got to be the best in your own space, the best in your own house, be the best in your own town, the best in your region, be the best in your own nation and then you become the best in the world. This is really about not quitting!

A client of ours has been searching for the right premises to run her own dog kennels and have her family home on the same premises for the past 5 years, as she is also a mum and a wife she defined all aspects of what she wanted and needed. Over the past 5 years, she has been committed to searching and not only continued to look, but she has also continued to educate herself, successfully run her own dog grooming business from home and successfully partnered up with another, running their own dog rescue. She didn't give up because she hadn't found the right premises, she continued to search and used her time in between to gain knowledge and experience. 5 years later she is just about to complete the sale of her house and the purchase of her new home combined with dog kennels. She understood that it could be a lengthy process, she had made an agreement with herself that she would continue to look regardless of how long. Now she is taking on the dog kennels as requested from herself; she had asked herself if she was prepared to commit to these dogs 24/7, she researched what it takes and continued to work in accordance to what she had asked for, which will be explained in the next chapter.

So if somebody says, you know you have got to be really committed, there like, what do you mean? Well, you have got to be really focused, well, what does that mean? Well, you have to have a tunnel vision, what does that mean? It means you don't allow yourself to have any other distractions, oh, right, how do I take the distractions away? You don't; it's called ***self-discipline***, when you really want something you don't allow anything to get in your way and you definitely don't allow others opinions to distract what you believe you can do.

Where your attention goes, energy flows and grows.

Maybe you knew you weren't going to read this book in one day, so you needed to be committed to getting to the other end of this book, you probably knew you weren't going to finish reading this before you finished drinking your drink, you knew you couldn't watch it, so you said to yourself, I'm going to give this amount of time, my mind, my energy and my resources and I'm going to trust and believe that it's got something valuable in there for me. I trust this person and where they come from, I've got confidence that they can help and guide me, I know it's going to take me maybe 4 weeks just to consume, I know that I'm probably going to have to go through it again and read the entire book twice, You're committed!

Also think about the above, and what other things you can do that fits your personality and helps you to commit and move forward, whether it's talking about them, sharing these requests that you have made to yourself, creating accountability with other people, It might be that you tell people what you are doing and what time scale you are trying to do it in and ask for what help and assistance they can give you and by doing that you must have committed to some degree because of the fact you are telling other people about it. We suggest making a vision board out of the things you have defined, maybe if you haven't already, then create a Pinterest account - depending on what scale they are, the further away these things are, the more you might be inclined to use something to help visualise it, so something you would like to have happened in 6 months' time, you might want to stick it on a Pinterest Board, if it's something for next week, make sure the detail of that is down on paper. If it's something on a year or 2 years, then it needs to be something that you can go back to and you can fuel your vision and realise how close or how far, or where you are in relation to accomplishing things and there are lots of things to accomplish on the way. It isn't just this one giant leap into having that thing, it is self-driven, the people who want a Ferrari, don't go from not driving at all and not having a license to a full on Ferrari ownership, they come to learn how to drive, so they experienced driving cars, maybe buy a house first, there are a few things that they will do before having a Ferrari, you need somewhere to put it, so again it's part and parcel.

What Doing Commit Looks Like - Exercise:

Here are some factors that you need to go and evaluate relative to the things you are thinking about becoming committed to…

Step One - Make sure you understand how long this could take

Make sure you know the full gambit of what's involved. All challenges must be laid down. You can't commit to something if you don't know how long it's going to take - people divorce because they don't actually know what it takes to stay committed, they don't understand the time scale involved and how to overcome the challenges. Go and find out how long it could take in the worst case, in the best case and maybe even middle case scenario, find out how long it normally takes, find out what it takes in one of the most wonderful instances of it happening and find out in the longest iteration of it ever happening, how long could that take? So if you could write a book in a week or you could write it in 8 months, or you could write it in two years, would you still commit to it in the worst case scenario of actually trying to do something in two years? Maybe you thought you could do it in 5 weeks, oh, you would commit to it if it was 5 weeks? But if it was 8 months, it's now no longer a commitment? What changed? The commitment time, which means, time can change a commitment. Take time to think about it.

Notes on how long you will need to be committed.

_____
_____
_____
_____
_____
_____
_____

Step Two - Research what it takes.

Don't downplay what's going to be involved, Make sure you can visualise and breakdown in detail all of the challenges and accept that you're going to do everything you can to get around or over all of the known issues or lengthy timescale that's down.

Do enough research, so you know what's going on and then ask yourself whether or not you're still up for it. There are some factors that you need to go and evaluate relative to the things you are thinking about being committed to. Consider these factors and note them, ask yourself questions and then at the end of that, you'll probably find that you've got a stronger resolve.

Notes on factors to be considered

_____
_____
_____
_____
_____
_____
_____
_____

Step Three - Are you still prepared to commit?

Once you've got all of this detail and you've not downplayed or underplayed it, you have not underestimated it, you then can make a conscientious decision that you are going to go through whatever the amount of time it's going to require and through over and above everything and once you're making that decision you're not just deciding to have it now, you've decided after you know everything that's involved in it you're still going to go for it.

List of the things I have consciously decided and agreed with myself to commit to.

_____
_____
_____
_____
_____
_____
_____

Step Four - Fully Committed?

Now that you have researched everything that it is going to take, are you prepared to do all those things to get it?

Are you prepared to wait the amount of time it's going to take to be able to do it?

If you have answered Yes to both questions, congratulations you've just done a great job of committing because despite what you know could be involved you believe that you can do it, you have the confidence that you will make it and you trust in you to stay grounded and to do it, and that combination of things, with you knowing what's really involved just lead to you actually committing. Now you decided against all the odds to do it and you were okay with the timeline. Congratulations to you!

> *"Commitment means staying loyal to what you said you were going to do long after the mood you said it in has left you"* - Muscleforlife.com

"There are only two options regarding commitment: you're either in or you're out. There's no such thing as life in between."
- Pat Riley

CHAPTER 6

Step 4 - Operate

What You Need To Know:

Now you have completed step 3 and you are committed, it's time to operate in accordance with what you have committed too. Operate is all about behaviour, it's how you act, it's how you think, and it's how you speak. Operate is directly related to what we do in relation to what we have asked for, we have to operate in alignment with what we ask and our behaviour is just as powerful as our thinking, just because you said that you're going to do something, it doesn't mean you're going to do it. Your behaviour shows you if you are in alignment with your thoughts, actions and words.

For those who believe in God they will pray for things, they might say "Please God, let me have peace today, let me have a nice calm peaceful and wonderful afternoon", then they get up, jump in their car and blast the most aggressive and angry rap music, start driving aggressively, as fast as they can, cutting people up left right and center, get into an argument with someone; get out of the car and punch them in the face! Well this person is not operating in alignment with what they asked for, they haven't thought peaceful thoughts, they didn't introduce things in their life to help them along with it, they didn't put themselves in calm frame of mind, they choose to listen to aggressive music, they choose to get in their car and drive out of control, they choose to get out and punch someone in the face. I know this is a harsh and unrealistic example however it is a great example of someone operating out of alignment with what they just asked for and we are also saying in small things, we could be making exactly the same BIG error and working against what we asked for.

Many people seem to make this mistake in many things that they want, If we're asking and saying "I really want to be much better at doing this thing" but you didn't go and research it, you didn't go and YouTube it and watch videos about it, you didn't take yourself to workshops and try and learn about it and you didn't even connect with others that are doing it, then do you think that you're working in accordance with what you have asked for? No, you're working out of accordance with what you have asked for!

What You Need To Do - Actions:

Do everything that aligns you with what you asked, if there is anything you can do to help it along then do it, if you can research it then research it, if you can find it, then find it, if you can connect with someone, connect with them. Think it, Speak it, Do it.

It is very important that you **LIVE** in accordance with what you have asked for. **THINK** in accordance with what you have set out for, **TALK** in accordance with what you have set out for and **DO** in accordance with what you have set out for.

> *"There's a wonderful old Italian joke about a poor man who goes to church every day and prays before the statue of a great saint, begging, "Dear saint - please, please, please...give me the grace to win the lottery." This lament goes for months. Finally, the exasperated statue comes to life, looks down at the begging man*

and says in weary disgust. "My son - please, please, please...buy a ticket."

If someone says "I want to be able to have a successful business" the next thing is to start behaving like you're going to have a successful business - It means You will need to go and start studying, you will need to go and get your accounting information done, you will need to start making positive movements towards it, as if you were going to get it, there is no point just thinking and talking about it, as your missing the doing part, which won't actually get you very far!

"Activity finishes the miracle process of turning nothing into something" - *Jim Rohn*

Examples and Analogies:

If somebody was training to win a hundred meters at the Olympics, their explanation of it wouldn't be you have just got to feel like you're gonna win it, that would not go down, they would turn around and say to you, I am aiming to win, so I am going to prepare like a champion, I am going to do specific exercises and follow a specific nutrition plan to get me in the best position to receive the win. This is almost like project planning; a project planner does the following things, they will understand first what the objective of the project is, what they are trying to achieve. They would say, "We need to have this very clear, so we don't lose sight of what we are trying to achieve", they will then start to work out the next thing, which Will be the key objectives to the overall objectives as well, and then they will say, on the way to this there is going to be some milestones, the key milestones would be...

If you're building a house a couple of milestones will be, the day that they knocked down the existing building, that's a milestone, there are lots of things that lead up to getting to that point, but the Milestone of knocking the existing building down is a real result of a combination of previous things, probably the next big milestone is not necessarily getting the rubbish cleared, important as it is, the next Milestone would be the laying of the foundation, it's a milestone because until that piece happens, you cannot do anything else, you cannot make any more progress until that milestone is hit.

When they say, "what about the rubbish being cleared,' well that might not be a milestone because there might actually be sufficient space, and you can still be ordering other things, and it's not going to stop the progress of anything else. If the foundation has not been laid down, nothing else can be done; you can't start laying bricks because the foundation isn't there. If they don't make that milestone everybody else on the calendar is going to have to be moved, if you missed the Foundation by three days everybody's service is now going back by at least 3 days, so this roadmap is starting to build up, what they then do is get a sequencing schedule part. Now they can look at the whole thing and then go right, for us to build a house, what are we going to need to do? Everybody starts pitching in; you start to see there are a lot of different tasks and at that point, you start to get into sequencing which one needs to go first? All of the stuff gets put into order, which one happens next.

After they have been sequenced, they're then scheduled to what date, how long is it going to take to do, and at this point you have everything that is involved in doing it, and after putting them in the right order you now start asking the questions, how long is it going to take to do each one of these things and project plan starts to emerge, they start to see what the time plan is going to be to get this thing done, because everything that's in it, you can see what order they're in, you can see how long they're going to take and now you get a project plan which is effectively a work breakdown structure, breaking down everything that is involved and putting a time on it. The reason this is important, is, if you were to start thinking, acting speaking and behaving like you're about to accomplish whatever it is you ask for, you would need to in your own mind made something like a work breakdown structure so you know what you should be doing and working accordingly to getting it.

So when we say operate differently, we mean, thinking differently, acting differently, and doing both of these things constantly. Also, it means we're going to have to start talking differently, we don't talk in a negative context, and we talk in a positive context about it. Don't just hope it, and don't just believe it, Know it. It is actually so much more likely to be when we do speak of it in a positive and knowing way. Things are not going to go your way if you are doubting the process. To further our analogy, have you ever seen anybody who's trying to get a promotion and they want to move up into management? It is usually said to them, for them to be a manager, they're going to have to start behaving like there already a manager before they get a promotion. What do they mean? First of all, you're going to have to start thinking like one; you're going to have to start thinking of the team, not just you, you're going to have to start thinking of the department and thinking about the company and the company's reputation because managers have that responsibility. A manager is not just thinking, "Well this is my job, and this is what I do, nothing more and nothing less!" There thinking actual changes, they start talking differently, they start voicing things in a completely different way, and they start behaving differently. They start turning up before anybody else turns up, and they don't tend to leave until the last of the work is done. Now whether that's correct or not correct, the fact is, this is what we know and understand to be the path of a manager. I remember going in, and my managers were there before I got there, the managers start at 9, and my shift would start at 8 and I Would get in literally 2 minutes to 8, and they were already there to greet me, maybe offer me a drink, the point is the manager would look after me making sure I started my day right. When at the end of the day I would be like, "Right, it's 5.25, my shift finished at 5; I'm out!" The manager would still be there to tell me, I did a great job and to wish me a great evening. I would often think, wow, he was here before me and is still here after I have left. If something comes in last minute the manager won't leave it until the next day, the manager would get somebody straight onto it, because the manager is thinking appropriately, speaking accordingly and acting appropriately, that really means there operating differently and there operating in alignment with everything that they have defined, that they've demanded and that they're committed to. Now they're actually moving with it!

We can say how we mean something, it makes no difference, because the reality is, there is a result that comes from some of the things we may have chosen, you can't ask for something without having consequences, whether perceived good or bad, you have got to be prepared to face up to what it's gonna mean. I'm sure when Usain Bolt decided he wanted to be the Olympic champion triple times around and wanted all the fame that went with it, he probably didn't want them following him absolutely all the time and now they're following him all the time, even when he's off doing naughty stuff that society says he shouldn't be doing!

When we say someone didn't realise, is that because we think 'oh, I just didn't know'! Or is it because actually you didn't go far enough realizing, the what's and the why's, the details, what it's going to take or shall I say, what's it's really going to take. Actually get on and do it, what do we mean by that? When we look at our actual exercises to do, we are saying, if you want to become better at something, the doing part means to get the book, watch the film, try it out, connect with people, get in the community, literally immerse yourself in moving forward towards your goal. So working in alignment is a big piece of getting what you want. This is about doing things that will bring you closer to what you have asked for. Do things that are in alignment with what you asked. If you have asked for peace, don't be aggressive, don't start listening to aggressive music. Think of the minute details of the things that collectively add up to doing things and to getting what you want.

What Doing Operate Looks Like - Exercises

Think in accordance with what you have set out for, do it in a positive context using these Practical Steps:

Step One

With one of the things you wrote down before, list 5 active positive steps that you could take which will bring you closer to getting what you want. Someone says "I really want to drive!" but they haven't even applied for their theory test however they continue to say "I really want to drive, but it isn't happening!" So they could start by downloading the theory book and start studying, that would be a positive step towards getting what they want and would also mean, is working in alignment with what they asked for.

1.

_____

_____

2.

_____
_____

3.

_____
_____

4.

_____
_____

5.

_____
_____

Step 2

Most people might not really evaluate the true impact of what they're really asking for. They might not be able to handle what they're asking for. Maybe you're asking for a business to become really successful, developing and growing, can you handle being rushed off your feet, being demanding of all the time? List 5 Details, Go far enough, realising the what's, the why're the details, what it's really going to take!

1.

_____
_____
_____
_____

2.
_____
_____
_____
_____

3.
_____
_____
_____
_____

4.
_____
_____
_____
_____

5.
_____
_____
_____
_____

Step 3

Actually get on and do it, what do we mean by that? When we look at our exercises to do we are saying; if you want to become better at something, the doing part means, get the book, watch stuff related to it, try it out, connect with people, get in the community, literally immerse yourself in moving towards your goal.

CHAPTER 7

Step 5 - Appreciate

What you need to know:

Now that you have Defined what you want, you have Demanded the details, you are committed to making it happen, you are operating in accordance to what you have committed to, and now it's time to appreciate the process and life itself. As individuals we're like little spheres of energy, our energy can go up and down, if we are putting so much effort into a particular area, what we have to be mindful of is that we are going to be depleting our energy store quite rapidly, if we're going to channel so much into things. We must take a moment and a step back and appreciate the things that we already have and that we have available to us, finding that, the process is almost like a re-energisation. So we have to take a moment to take stock of the things that we do have.

> *"Appreciate life even if it's not perfect. Happiness is not the fulfilment of what we wish for, but an appreciation of what we have"* - Picturequotes.com

We need to appreciate that we have a roof over our head, even appreciate that we have a bathroom and a toilet to use, even toilet paper to use as there are many people in the world that do not have the luxury of these facilities and are using holes in the ground and leaves to clean themselves. Even appreciate the fact that we have food to eat that causes our bodies to use the toilet! We must be very mindful of our position and begin to appreciate all of the different aspects of our life that are on track so that we can see the fact; we are generally winning. If we can perceive ourselves as being successful and perceive ourselves as generally winning, we are going to feel significantly more motivated to be able to stay on that winning track and push through with everything we have mentioned previously in the 4 sections.

This is a cycle which is recommended for us to be in on a regular basis, we're not saying do a monthly appreciation plan we're talking about appreciating everything, appreciating the fact that we have got life and we have got people around us, people that we can love and people that love us, and we've got reasons to be able to do things and enjoy things, all of those things appreciate them! Make sure you appreciate the progress you have made so far.

> *"Trade your expectation to appreciation and the world changes instantly"* - Tony Robbins

If we don't start appreciating the fact that we're here and what we have access to, then you are missing the point, as Steve Jobs says "If there is one thing that we can all guarantee in life; we're all going to die! We cannot escape this". So we need to appreciate every moment that we have.

Be mindful that we're going to pass one day, so are the people around you; you know what? Drink them in, drink in the fact that even if they're not going to pass on anytime soon, the fact that they're changing, everybody's changing, appreciate your children as they are at this age now because they're only going to be this age once, appreciate your partner as they are right now, because they're going to change, endure the people you love, appreciate exactly who they are in this moment because time will pass and if we do not appreciate them then we're missing the point.

Right now only streets away from you or maybe in the next town, there is somebody living a life which you could not even begin to imagine, they don't know if they're going to make it to tomorrow. Their hustling minute after minute, hour by hour, they're involved in street gangs, crime, drugs, etc. doing the most de-praised things to be able to provide for themselves and those around them and they may well have lost all those who mattered to them, all their friends, the people they went to school with don't know them now, their families have disconnected from them and disowned them and their literally on their own in this world, not knowing if tomorrow is going to be a day that they will get to see.

There is so much opportunity in the world if you are open to it however you've got to be strong to be open to the benefits, you've got to be ready, you can't be shut off, angry, worried and constipated if you will. Constipated with the problems of the world that you can't even shit out the badness you've closed yourself up; you can't even get rid of the toxins because you have shut yourself off!

There's a world of opportunities; we need to start breathing in and appreciating the natural beauty of our planet, the flowers that we see, the rain that falls that helps our flowers and grass grow because there are people that don't get to do that. A child has just had their legs blown off in Syria; there are many children and adults that are experiencing the sound and smell of bombs on a daily basis. They would love to just walk down the road and see grass and not fear the raffle of a gun, and that's real right now.

If we don't start appreciating the fact that we're here and what we have access to, then again you are missing the point, so don't focus and look at what's going wrong, wasting this precious life by moaning about the problems of the world, spend your time doing the things that you love and want to do, appreciate, love and respect yourself and be the best version of you that you can possibly be at every moment. Acknowledge what's wrong and be the change you want to see.

> *"You can't live a positive life with a negative mind"* - Urlaw™

We need to appreciate where we are, what we have and what we can do for the rest. Say thank you for the food you have to eat, the roof over your head, constant appreciation of everything that you are getting to enjoy and you are having. The cycle is you actually implementing this on a daily basis, not even on a daily basis, on an hourly basis. Get into a mindset, a state of appreciation on a constant basis. Appreciate the fact that your body knows how to breathe without you having to instruct it to. Appreciate your friends, appreciate what you do every day, appreciate who your family are. Let appreciation become something that you do.

How do you appreciate? Do you realise when you are eating food, there is a lot of people that can't even get food? They can't even get water, they have to walk for miles to get a little water and we can just turn on our taps and there it is! We need to start appreciating who we are, what we have and what we can do for the rest of the world.

> *You think your life is bad? Think of others and you may realise that it is just your perspective mind that is bad. Change your perspective and your life will change.*

We need to think bigger than ourselves. Appreciation is a really big part of it because it puts our own problems into perspective, it makes our small problems like paying for a water bill, be like, "hold on, I'm lucky that I am even in a place where I've got a water bill to pay."

Let me ask you, how would you like to be remembered once you have passed away? Would you like to be remembered as the person who said they would and never did? Or the person that said they would and always did? Just know you have the power to influence and you can go out and give the best of what you have got, it's more likely that you will accomplish what you set out to do. It's a change in position of language; it's that juxtaposition of thinking that is ultimately different, it's the difference between absolute winners and losers.

Let me ask you, how much do you think Formula One is physiological? It's completely physiological, yes you have to have talent. However, if you don't believe you can go faster, you won't have the bravery to commit to going faster. It takes balls and belief however nothing is too small and nothing is too big, it's all perspective.

> *"If you change the way you look at things, the things you look at change"* - *Wayne Dyer*

What you need to do - Actions

The moment you can begin to appreciate, you're going to start realising benefits that are outside of what you even asked for, you will find relationships with your family members will improve, your relationship with your partner will improve because you're appreciating them and the things that they actually did go out of their way to do. It will change the way that you feel about people and it will change your perspective of life which is the beginning of all life improving and perspective is really important when working towards things that are coming up but are not here right now and looking at each opportunity that you have and looking at everything positive that has to lead up to it.

> *"The way to develop the best that is in a person is by appreciation and encouragement"* - Charles Schwab

Examples and Analogies

Being able to appreciate things effectively gives us perspective and perspective is really important when working towards things that are coming up but are not here right now.

To give you an idea of what's going on with appreciation, I would like you to consider a story with me. Imagine, someone who's trying to improve their body, dramatically change their body, there working out, there drinking at least 8 liters of water a day, compared to the 2 liters previous trying to change their body. There doing fitness training, lifting weights, they're doing cardio, they're doing everything right, there eating all the right stuff, drinking the right drinks. 5-6 weeks down the line, if they had not been appreciating all the small wins of the things that they have done, they would lose perception very quickly and end up failing, they wouldn't be able to foresee the reality of everything that is going on and would get on the scales, see that there 2 pounds heavier; demoralising! End of the project, end of the show.

Or that same person could have been appreciating all of the small wins that they were making all of the positives that were coming out, everything positive that has to lead up to it. The fact that because there drinking more water they would have a larger water percentage and they would actually have a larger muscle density because of the fitness training, the cardio, despite the fact that their weight didn't even go down, didn't stay the same, it went up, but actually their waist is half an inch smaller because there was less fat but more muscle so they would weigh more, their behaviour changed, their eating more healthily, their feeling more energised, their feeling a whole lot healthier, they fit into their clothes better, they can walk further, they can run further they sleep better and actually when they stepped on the scales because they have been appreciating they realised there water attention had gone up, their fat mass had gone down, so when they see that their 2 pounds heavier they celebrated rather than cried, they were joyous, because of their appreciation, people gain more perspective and see things for what they really are when appreciating.

So without appreciation, we can lose sight of the overall picture of where we really are at. You're probably making a lot more progress than you think you are, but if you are judging success by the result, you're going to get disheartened. Can you see if they didn't appreciate the smaller things, the smaller achievements and the smaller wins and they weren't in the habit of doing that on a regular basis they would lose sight of all the focus that they had, it would jeopardise them actually making it. Have you heard the saying "Stay hungry, stay foolish?" This means, stay hungry for information and consider yourself to be foolish if you will so that you can always learn and continue appreciating everything that's about and around you.

What Doing Appreciate Looks Like - Exercise

For the next 21 days, we would like you to do some very specific tasks every day. In the morning we would like you to take stock and appreciate a bunch of things that have happened that have got you through the morning.

Positively reflect throughout the day. Put it on your calendar as a little 5-minute exercise to take a moment to reflect all the good stuff. Call it the 'Good Reflect' Brand it, make it your own, have it in your calendar, get an alert, so if you have a smartphone, you will feel it vibrate, giving you a reminder saying; you wanna take a moment to appreciate everything that has happened today? This is about making a definitive shift in the way you are looking at life.

Step One

In the morning by the time you have actually had some food, think of everything decent that has happened. Appreciate the fact that you got a good night's rest. Appreciate that you got out of a nice warm bed, went to the bathroom and washed your face with running water, that you went to the kitchen and had something to eat, which means you have the ability to make that environment, as you're living it.

We have provided you with enough space below to write a handful of the things you can appreciate. The space provided is only for the first few days, and then you can refer to the notebook you bought at the beginning of this process.

Monday Morning

1. _____
2. _____
3. _____
4. _____
5. _____

Tuesday Morning

1. _____
2. _____
3. _____
4. _____
5. _____

Wednesday Morning

1. _____
2. _____
3. _____
4. _____
5. _____

Step two

Then carry on with your day, the next time that you do it is around midday or lunchtime take 5 minutes to stop and look back and appreciate all of the things that you were able to accomplish in the morning. You made it to the office safely? Did you get the train no problems? You made it; you solved people's problems? You made things happen alright? You got things organised, you spoke to a loved one and it's all good you're ticking things off? Are you making progress? You're doing well; today is a day you brought some goodness into the world for some people, so your sunny side up let's go! What are you going to do this afternoon? It's almost like you're a superhero if you think about it, you start feeling incredible, you've given people help, you found great solutions, you've guided people, you're on fire but because we do it every day on a regular, we just think it's normal and were skipping amazing things like there nothing. Take note, appreciate it.

Monday Lunchtime

1. _____
2. _____
3. _____
4. _____
5. _____

Tuesday Lunchtime

1. _____
2. _____
3. _____
4. _____
5. _____

Wednesday Lunchtime

1. _____
2. _____
3. _____
4. _____
5. _____

Step Three

Do the same at the end of the day, when you're in bed, avoid the negative stuff and just focus and appreciate all the decent stuff that happened throughout your day, perceive everything great that happened in the day, everything that you enabled to do, to give or to receive and to really put yourself in a great place. Now if you want to be a real boss about this and move into a slightly more advanced position then maybe get your notepad out and write an appreciation list of your whole day putting them all up together and maybe read through them before you go to sleep. Do this for a week and see how you feel then do it for another week and see how the quality of your appreciation goes, seeing if you are beginning to appreciate more of what is going on around you, by the time you reach the end of week 2 review it at the end of each week and maybe even read it back to yourself.

After 2 weeks, now try and make it to 21 days, if you can do 21 days of this, they say that actually, 21 days of doing the same thing consecutively helps you form a habit so try and do this for 21 days and after 21 days, see if you can keep going. Try and make this part of your everyday life, for the rest of your life!

For now, you can use the space below to start you off.

Monday BedTime

1. _____
2. _____
3. _____
4. _____
5. _____

Tuesday BedTime

1. _____
2. _____
3. _____
4. _____
5. _____

Wednesday BedTime

1. _____
2. _____
3. _____
4. _____
5. _____

"Appreciation can make a day, even change a life. Your willingness to put it into words is all that is necessary" -
Margaret Cousins

CHAPTER 8

Step 6- Wait

What you need to know

Now this is the last step to this system, and probably the most important step, you have Defined what you want, Demanded what you want, Committed to what you want, Operating in accordance to what you want, appreciated life on a daily basis including the smalls wins along the way and Now it's Time to Wait! Patience is the key here, you have planted your seeds and now it is time to let them sow. We want you to enjoy the process of what you have defined, and we want you to enjoy all of the phases of the unfolding of this. You have to wait for the seed to sow. You can't water a plant and then all of a sudden the plant just sprout's 5 inches, you must have patience. This is about being pragmatic; it's about being realistic and having patience without freaking out that it hasn't happened yet.

So you knew how long it was going to take for some of these things to happen, now there are so many things you can literally appreciate whilst you're waiting, you know it's going to come into play, you know you're going to experience it, so appreciate where you are right now in relation to it and enjoy the journey to it. What is the one thing that you have to wait for and there is nothing you can do apart from wait? Having a baby! You cannot speed this process up; no human being can make it happen faster, it takes up to nine months. You can have intercourse with nine different women and create 9 babies, but you can't get more women for the process of having a baby, you can't say, right! Give me 9 women I want a baby next month; some things take time.

Wait gives you the opportunity, the time, to look back at the stuff that you have been doing, and know that you are not just idly waiting, you can recognise that you have done things to help the progression and when people are waiting for a baby, they don't just say "well, that was that we just wait" they do all sorts of things to help it along, not to make it happen faster but to help, so when it does arrive, that it arrives in the best way possible! People sing to their baby, talk to their baby, rub their belly, attend antenatal classes, they eat healthily, visit the doctors regularly, they take the right vitamins. They do everything to help them along the process; they change what they're doing, they don't do so much stuff or anything that's going to jeopardise their pregnancy. There are indeed things to do, and there is a lot more to having a baby than meets the eye, you just make sure you don't do anything that will jeopardise it. A pregnant Lady does not doubt the process; she will work in accordance with the process, the same stands with everything you want in life.

You can also think of it like planting corn, part of the process of planting corn is preparing the soil, to progress in this matter you should understand that the corn has to be placed within the soil. Common sense should lead you to realise that throwing a tantrum and demanding it to grow will not solve your goal for it to grow, right? So with anything and everything in life that is the case, so there is no point in wasting time feeling disappointed, instead, realise your mistakes in that time and get to understand the fact that it needs to germinate inside the soil with you putting effort to help it grow! At first, there will be no outcome but patience is key in this instance because you must wait for your hard work to pay off (which might take a while, but it will happen). So, in the beginning, you may get a bit agitated, but you'll learn the unfolding process which will help you become successful. The result will be something you will cherish.

Another analogy to help clarify what wait is, if you set yourself a target of saying you are going to travel and see Brazil in 9 months' time; getting locked up in 6 months for 3 years, pretty much gets in the way of that, right! Researching online the best places to visit whilst in Brazil and things of alike would be a better thing to do and will not jeopardise you travelling to Brazil in 9 months' time.

What you need to do (Actions)

What wait is not, it's not just literally, I'm just sitting here and I'm not doing anything, there are plenty of things to do along the way to it becoming. Think about the analogy we just gave of someone who's having a baby, the parents know, that did what they needed to do to start the process off and now they don't just say "oh well, that's that!, I'll see you in nine months!" they constructively work towards the wonderful gift they are going to get in nine months, in the full knowledge that they can't go and get some extra women to make the baby come quicker or anything like that, they know, it's going to be nine months and then they do everything that they can to make sure when it arrives, they're ready for it! Like we were saying they will be educating themselves, the type of parent they are going to be, they will be making sure they know how to handle it when they have it, they go to education classes, they start finding out about children and how they grow, what they need, their dietary requirements, What they would need to do if they decided on a home birth, water birth or give birth in hospital and if they decided on giving birth in the hospital, they would pack a bag closer to the time in preparation for spending time in hospital and their bag wouldn't be just a change of clothes for the parent, there would also be clothes and nappies for their newborn.

It's funny that we don't look at everything from that same perspective; we get angry and disappointed because we haven't seen the results and then give up. Could you imagine if every pregnant women become angry because the pregnancy test said she is pregnant and then the doctors confirmed it and after 2 weeks throws a tantrum that her baby was still in her belly and because she was yet to see it, hold it and touch it, started doubting that there will even be a baby, demanding to have a scan on a weekly basis because she doubts there's a baby!

So as we just mentioned, Waiting is not sitting on your arse doing Nothing; waiting is still constructively moving forward and getting yourself ready. So if you wanted to own a Ferrari in 12 months, You need to probably drive a Ferrari, it's going to be in your interest to drive something at least as powerful as a Ferrari beforehand, maybe go out with a couple of people in their Ferrari's maybe try and pay to go on a Supercar day 2 or 3 times, so by the time you get yours, you don't do what happened to that guy in the paper the other day, he got a brand new Maclaren and he didn't even get 25 minutes away from the dealerships and he put it in a tree. So the time he was waiting for the car, he waited months to get that car, and when he got it, he crashed it, he totally wasted his wait period, he squandered the time he had to wait by not preparing himself to drive such a powerful car and the end result was a brand new car wrapped around a tree. Don't squander the waiting period.

Appreciate all of the progressive steps that you have made towards getting this far. And then continue to do what we have mentioned before about operating in accordance with it; we said you have got to work with it rather than against it. Well that is what you are doing when you are waiting, we taught you how to do it, we even said when to do it but now we are clarifying even more that operate phase that kind of happens while you're waiting, you continue to work in accordance with what you set yourself out for, what you asked for, what you demanded, you really done your research, really found out what you would have to do, what it really required, you committed to it, you knew most of what would be involved, you prepared, you focused on the journey, and now don't mess it up by becoming impatient.

Examples and Analogies:

If you are out of a job and you decide to re-profile your CV and you literally just finished doing your CV and thought, I know exactly what roles I need to go for and you've gone online, you've committed to a few different agencies, you've sent your CV in, you did it all by 11 am and it's now 1 pm and you're like why haven't I got a job yet, I've done everything they said, I've applied to the agencies, I've re-profiled my CV, I've put it online, what more do they want? Why haven't I got a job yet? Surely I should have one, they told me this is the ballast CV, this is top 100%, this is going to bring it home, why hasn't it happened? You know what this doesn't work, forget this stupid CV, I wish I hadn't wasted my time going through this nonsense. What's the one key piece that is missing here? PATIENCE! You haven't waited for the results to happen of what you have done, you've done something that's CAUSE, the EFFECT is the market will respond once the market has had a chance to have a look, once the market has contacted all the people that have got jobs available, who can give you a job. Every single company that is in recruitment, unless they specifically have a recruitment team, that they're so big that they actually have a huge team of people doing recruitment, then it's going to take time. Just think, every company that has somebody interviewing you for employment, interviewing is not there job, their day job is their actual day job, not interviewing people, so when they have 20, 30, 40 emails coming on with people's C.V's in there, how fast do you think they are opening that, on top of doing their actual job? It's going to take time; this is about pragmatic. This is about being Pragmatic; it's about being realistic.

> *"Two things define you. Your patience when you have nothing, and your attitude when you have everything"* - Zig Ziglar

Somebody can't be sitting in London today thinking, "You know what, I want to be in Australia today and then be in Australia today! No can do! There is no plane that is going to get you to Australia today, you can want that as much as you like, you're not getting there today, you can maybe get there tomorrow but you cannot get there today. It is impossible, Law of Attraction is not going to get you to Australia today, even if Concord was still flying, it would not have enough fuel to get you there. So hold out for throwing your toys out of the pram, be patient and wait for your seeds to sow. As we said, you can't water a plant and then all of a sudden be like, Oh look at this, it's all just coming out, it's grown 5 inches in 5 seconds! Everything comes to you at the right time. Be patient and trust the process.

> *"Patience is not the ability to wait, but the ability to keep a positive attitude while waiting"* - Unknown

You need to define what it is that you're going to or want to try and get to, you pretty much make sure you've requested and authorised yourself to go and get it by demanding the details of it, then you need to commit to doing it, then you need to actually have association with what you have defined then you have to even appreciate everything that has gone right so far and then stick to everything you've done and wait for the results, if you took one of these steps out of the example that we have given, then you're not going to make it. If you don't appreciate everything that you have done to control the situation that you have done until this point and say forget it, I'm just going to forget it and move on, if you don't do the operate part of act, think and speak then you will lose confidence, faith and power, if you don't commit then that's obvious what will happen, without defining it, you're never going to make it anyway.

> *"Even if you're on the right track, you get run over if you just sit there"* - Will Rogers

What Doing Wait Looks Like - Exercises:

Keep remembering the baby analogy and look at the previous exercise of somebody who's trying to work out. Do you think it's equally important for someone who's working out to have patience? If they don't have patience with their results, they're going to give up! That's why people subscribe for 3 months, 6 months or 9 months transformation programs, in that time they have to have patience, imagine after week one they demand to see full results, and because they don't, they give up.

Patience is key, you have got to keep doing it, believe me, if you keep lifting weights and eating right you are going to have muscles. Imagine someone starts freaking out "hey! When are these muscles going to arrive? I've looked in the letterbox, I've seen the postman coming, where are my muscles!?" Sounds ridiculous right? Why do we start thinking that things in life work differently? They don't, it is a game of waiting and how constructive we are in that time is going to show how successful we will be in our endeavours, and we have to try and be comfortable in all our endeavours.

We need to know what the time scales are, when we are going to do something at the longest and then within that time scale, try and do everything we can to move progressively towards it, so if you want to have a driving license in a year's time, take lessons, take your theory test, think of things that you can do between now and then that's going to help, or A) you can just wait for the year to pass and hope that you pass your test without doing anything towards it, however as you know the chances are next to nothing of that happening and that would be the wrong kind of waiting or B) you can do the proper waiting where you work in accordance with it just like we said in operate.

Some people say, "oh, I'm never going to find a anybody, I'm never going to find a partner, and they stay indoors all day and all night, they don't socialise, in fact, with the technology and apps we have available at our fingertips they could actually stay indoors and still meet people, however, they chose just to watch T.V They don't go onto social network sites and interact with others, but they moan that they have wanted to meet someone for the last 6 months! Out of billions of people on planet earth, they think that there is nobody out there for them, not realising they actually have to operate in accordance with what you are wanting.

> *"Have patience no matter what the difficulty, no matter how dark the road ahead seems. For truly, with patience comes victory and with difficulty, relief follows close behind"*-
> Unknown

CHAPTER 9

Recap

Overall our aim was to make the whole concept of The Law of Attraction easier to digest, much more consumable, much easier to work with, helping people to think of it in a simple way. We hope that this book has given you the clarity you seek in relation to using The Law of Attraction as a powerful tool to get what you want out of life. We hope our simple 6 step system and have helped you on how to define and get clear on the things you want and the process it takes to achieve these things and experiences.

You now have a full step by step, section by section, practical guide to helping you apply The Law of Attraction in your life, you are now clear on what it is, what it's not and what it takes to make it work for you in all area of your life. Hopefully, we have cleared up any confusion in the areas where people found it to be a great concept, felt energised however struggled with actually putting it all into practice that you now feel re-energised and clear about how to put it into practice in anything you choose.

Leading us on to the next problem that we wanted to clear and clarify, which was people didn't really know where they were going, there was no order in which to do things, they even felt the things they needed to do, the actual tactics; they weren't too detailed, they were left with this feeling of not really knowing what to do next or what items to even take to try and do next.

We hope we have given you a clear strategy in moving forward, an overall roadmap and most importantly an order in which to do things and we hope we have fulfilled the actual tactics in which to do things in your everyday life and given full details that people felt were missing and hopefully you are feeling like you now know what to do next in any given area in your life.

People had also mentioned that it had created an element of fear within them and that fear was related to feeling out of control, like things were not in their hands, that this Law of Attraction had defined everything that happened in their past, and through all the information we have presented to you, that element of fear has been eliminated, knowing that you are in control and you are now aware that you can't just knock stuff straight off, this isn't about not acknowledging things that are negative and bad, it's not a blanket that gets thrown on top of stuff and gets covered away and put to the side, it's a tool for working out how to deal with them!

Let's have a Quick re-cap to what it takes to achieve the things you want.

- **Step 1 - Defining -** This section is the beginning of the mind training process, defining exactly what is it that you want specifically by writing down what you want, by listing in order of how soon you would like or need them to happen. Remember we said why we should write it down? Because through research, we found people who commit their thoughts to paper have a significantly higher success rate of achieving the things they have written down, remembering always to be very clear, as unclear thoughts will result in unclear results.

- ***Step 2 - Demanding*** - This section is about demanding, demanding the detail that makes it significantly more realistic. Remember, one of the reasons we saying to go into detail is because, if you care to dream it out, you may realise that you are focusing on something you don't actually want. So you need to be crystal clear, demanding more information about it and more information about why we want it, demanding yourself to know why demanding you to ask why and then demand that it happens! Once you have clarified this to yourself, you will start building the confidence to move forward.

- ***Step 3 - Commit*** - This whole section is about learning the meaning of commitment, understanding that this is something that you will be learning to do from yourself to yourself, by yourself and for yourself. So it's from you, by you, to you and for you, knowing there will be hurdles, and in some cases, the hurdles may appear to be impossible to overcome however with every problem there is a solution, so focus on the solution, not on the problem. We described commitment as a cake, remember the ingredients to our commitment cake? Having Trust, Belief and Confidence in yourself, there's got to be an honesty about realistically how much is required. Some people commit to something that they think is going to be easy and when they realise it's not, they give up. We believe you don't want to be that person that gives up!

- ***Step 4 - Operate*** - This section is all about behaviour, it's how you **Act,** it's how you **Think** and it's how you **Speak**. Operate is directly related to what we do in relation to what we have asked for, we have to operate in alignment with what we ask and your behaviour shows you if you are in alignment with your thoughts, actions and words. Remember it is very important that you LIVE in accordance with what you have asked for. THINK in accordance with what you have set out for, TALK in accordance with what you have set out for and DO in accordance with what you have set out for. So working in alignment is a big piece of getting what you want. This is about doing things that will bring you closer to what you have asked for by doing things that are in alignment with what you asked.

- **Step 5 - Appreciate -** This section is all about appreciating, taking a moment to step back and appreciate the things that we already have and that we have available to us now. Remembering to be very mindful of our position and begin to appreciate all of the different aspects of our life that are on track, so that we can see the fact we are generally winning. If we can perceive ourselves as being successful and perceive ourselves as generally winning, we are going to feel significantly more motivated to be able to stay on that winning track. Being able to appreciate things effectively gives us perspective and perspective is really important when working towards things that are coming up but are not here right now. Appreciating will change the way that you feel about people and it will change your perspective of life which is the beginning of all life improving and perspective is really important when working towards things that are coming up but are not here right now and Looking at each opportunity that you have and looking at everything positive that has to lead up to it so appreciate as often as possible.

Remember - if you can do 21 days of this, they say that actually, 21 days of doing the same thing consecutively helps you form a habit.

- **Step 6 - Wait -** This section is all about having patience, planting your seeds and allowing them to grow without getting frustrated and upset that you are yet to see your results of the seeds that have been planted by you. Remember the baby analogy? You cannot speed this process up; no human being can make it happen faster, it takes up to nine months. A pregnant Lady does not doubt the process; she will work in accordance with the process, the same stands with everything you want in life.

Remember we said, imagine if every pregnant woman become angry because the pregnancy test said she is pregnant and then the doctors confirmed it and after 2 weeks had a tantrum that her baby was still in her belly and because she was yet to see it, hold it and touch it, started doubting that there will even be a baby!

So as we just mentioned, Waiting is not sitting on your arse doing Nothing; waiting is still constructively moving forward and getting yourself ready and appreciating all the small wins in the process.

"We can achieve anything we focus on negative or positive; it's your choice to which you choose to consume your mind with."
Urlaw™

Well That's it, we hope we have brought value to your life and delivered what we promised to deliver through our research, personal life experiences of ourselves, friends, colleagues and through us using the same simple 6 step Urlaw™ system and principles to create and achieve this finished product that you have in your hands right now, it's worked wonders for us and it is now in your hands, helping you to achieve the great things you know you are capable of achieving!

Get to know you, work with you and give you the tools that you need to build the life you so deserve, take the system, use the system and using this tool will get you almost anything you want so let's put it to work and see what it can do for you!

We would appreciate you sending us your success stories so we can celebrate together!

Wishing you all the Love, Abundance, Health, Wealth and Success!

The Law of Attraction

NOTES

ANTHEA MORPHITIS

How Does The Law of Attraction Work? Questions and Answers

Q: *How does the Law of Attraction work?*

A: It works a lot like many other universal laws. One of the most common comparisons is that like attracts like. With the Law of Attraction, whatever thoughts and feelings your energy is emitting will determine the thoughts and energy that is returned to you in the form of experiences. It is always at work, which is why sometimes you attract more of what you don't want. The best way to describe it is to think of yourself as a magnet that attracts equal circumstances to bring about more of your current thoughts and emotions. If you are happy and feeling very grateful for what you have, the universe will respond by bringing you more to feel happy and grateful about. The Law of Attraction cannot break other laws of physics and our universe. Our feelings and thoughts create vibrations, which are emitted into our environment, attracting the things that we are determined to get.

Q: *Why are some Law of Attraction methods difficult for some people?*

A: Law of Attraction methods may be challenging due to two different reasons. The first happens when you don't believe that the method will work. You must believe that it will work for you. The second reason happens when people allow any of the ***LOA***

blockers to dominate their mind. These blockers include ***fear, doubt, negative thoughts and feelings, being ungrateful, selfish or unforgiving***, allowing negative people to get to you, allowing motivation to fade, giving up and having negative beliefs about what you are working towards and what it means to be abundant.

Q: How can I make sure that I am attracting wealth at all times?

A: By keeping an optimistic attitude and being determined to succeed in all aspects of your life, you will keep the Law of Attraction working for you and not against you. You must also shed limiting beliefs that you may have about yourself and receiving. The Law of Attraction is always working in your life, despite whether you want it to or not. So making it work to your benefit is very important.

Q: What is vibrational energy?

A: Vibrational energy is your aura. It is what makes up your emotions, intentions and thoughts. The frequency of your vibrational energy depends on your mood and what you want. Your vibrational energy acts as a signal to the universe. As your energy gives off this signal, the universe interprets it to bring you more of the same thoughts and moods you are experiencing. Think of vibrational energy as your communication line for ordering the experiences you desire.

Q: How will being thankful for what I have bring me more success?

A: Being thankful for what you already have is the key to attracting what you want with Law of Attraction. This type of attitude strengthens your vibrational energy and aligns it with that which you want to happen. Just learning to appreciate your life now will go a long way in bringing you more things to be thankful for.

Q: *How long does it take for things to come into my life?*

A: The Law of Attraction is constantly working in your life as long as you play an active role. There is no sudden marked beginning to when it begins working and there is no way to tell how quickly things will manifest into your life. The reason for this is due to the harmony in which all laws of the universe exist. They are all working together to create the world we know, but they cannot contradict each other. This creates an effect that is not magical, but practical. The longer you put your mind to something and back it up with passion, the more and more likely it will become a reality. Alternatively, if you give up on your desires before it has a chance to manifest, the universe will move on too. Only those that are determined to succeed and never give up will find their desires manifesting fully.

Q: *What can't I do utilizing the Law of Attraction?*

A: The Law of Attraction cannot be used to break other universal laws. For example, you won't be able to make a wish and instantly receive a check for a million pounds, or transport yourself to a vacation paradise in the blink of an eye. However, you will be able to create the conditions for you to live a life where you can afford to take vacations or do anything else that money can buy. It takes going through a process, but the foundation begins with believing what you want is possible and following the Urlaw™ System.

Q: *What does it mean to align yourself with what you want?*

A: This is all about feeling as if you already have what you want. Getting into alignment typically involves lots of practice, meditation techniques and daily affirmations to bring your subconscious mind into alignment with what you want. Experiencing the feelings associated with abundance, happiness and everything you want will align you with those things. The more you feel as if you have already received what you want, the easier it will be to have it.

Q: Can other people's intentions cause mine not to manifest?

A: This is a question that does not have a definite yes or no answer. It depends solely on the situation. If you don't believe that you have opposition, then you can continue to keep your goals on the right track. The moment doubt sets in about your abilities, or you feel that you have a chance at failure, those feelings can begin to manifest as well. The key is to have total faith that nothing will ever get in your way of accomplishing your dreams.

Q: Will the Law of Attraction make all of my wishes come true?

A: This is entirely up to you. If you gain full control over your positive energy and harness it correctly, you can make all of your wishes come true.

Q: Can I use the Law of Attraction even if I'm not sure it will work for me?

A: Yes, but you have to have faith in yourself. Almost everyone that has made the Law of Attraction work for them started out as skeptical as they come. It's not always easy to put your full faith into something right away. Thankfully, you don't have to when you use the Urlaw™ System and follow our guidance during this system. Simply use this system to the best of your abilities and that will be enough to get the ball rolling. Once you see your life changing before your eyes, all skepticism will be washed away.

www.ingramcontent.com/pod-product-compliance
Lightning Source LLC
Chambersburg PA
CBHW071021080526
44587CB00015B/2449